Stardust And Broken Dreams

Arianna Alakante

BookLeaf Publishing

Stardust And Broken Dreams

Presentation by *BookLeaf Publishing*

Web: www.bookleafpub.com

E-mail: info@bookleafpub.com

ISBN: 9789357212915

First edition 2023

To my Children,

Thank you for the honour of being your Muma, however unsuccessfully I do it.

I love you.

And Nathan, For continually showing up and inspiring me to reach further.

ACKNOWLEDGEMENT

To all those who either Sparked my heart flame,
Threw logs to keep her burning, or tried to
extinguish but ended up reminding me how
bright a flame I am.
And just quietly, Liam. Thanks Dude.

PREFACE

This Book came into being because it's one of the few things my sponsor told me to do and I listened.
And also because the best revenge is to eviscerate them in literature.

INDEX

A Magical Charlatan

What if I lied to make you leap,
what if I push to make you see,
what if I cry, so you don't feel alone.
What if all I do is to make you See you?
Take away the insipid childishness,
The veil of wisdomatic truth,
there behind lies a ruthless bear stripping away
at your core,
relating and responding without fear.
Why you ask would anyone do such a thing?
For You.
Because a you stripped bare is you anew,
without all the stupid beliefs that keep you from
the beautiful amazing human you are.
God sent me to you to unlock the treasure within
and you've got to mine
away the dirt so you know it exists in you,
but once you see the gift of your spectacular self
it's Up to You.
I am but a moment in time in your life and you
Won't even remember my name 10 years from
now 'cos it isn't about me…
It's about You.

Choices

If you capture a moment,
would it be fear or hope,
hate or love?
Would it be the fight or the calm,
the fire or the ashes?
Your strength or the battles end?
Would you recall your moment of tempest or
surrender?
Would you recall the light or the dark you
overcame?

Piece-by-piece you choose what defines you or
what refines you.

Will you allow bitterness to be the result of scars
or will they serve as a reminder of your tenacity
in battle?

What platter do you want to eat from -
Regret or Fortitude,
Sadness or Strength?

The meal you serve today will determine the
appetite of your tomorrow.
So eat well, my friends.

Hiding in Plain Sight

I'm not here to be loved, I'm here to show love,
I'm here to take the Slings And Arrows.
You misunderstand is always, no one will ever
love the whole me 'cos I'm not human,
I am an angel.
I died so long ago, I'm here, but I'm not here to
accomplish anything of this earth.
I'm here to introduce you to the real you.

I'm just visiting, not a permanent resident.
I come from love and I will return to love.
Someday I will expire, but I know, God knows I
love loving you.
shaking your silly constructed possibilities
when they are infinite - just like you.

I love the moment you realise you're a soul
having a human life and you can make it
anything you want.
It just takes sacrifice.
It always comes down to Sacrifice.
So I wonder sometimes when these books are
found if you call me mad, or believe that even
angels have human experiences, because we
need to know your pain to heal it.

Wants, Needs and Truths

I want to dance
I want to love
I want to be desired
I want to be special
I want to be loved
I want to laugh
I want to seek God
I want to be smart
I want to be intuitive
I want to inspire
I want to lead
I want to understand
I want to guide
I want to hear
I want to trust
I want to believe
I want to know
I want to risk
I want to fall
I want to know the next right action
I want to be healed
I want to be Fearless
I want to be me
I am free
I Am Alive
I am Me

The Voluptuous Mind

A journey through the voluptuous mind,
Brings a tragic disharmony one will find,
She is full of self yet never defined,
She yearns but never finds,
Her interest is piqued in all things divine,
She's adrift in every moment in time,
Occasionally her Tempest roars,
The Dollhouse collapses and the mind unwinds,
But she rises back up again,
And will hold you entranced,
For she is the voluptuous mind

True Love Dreams

Rolling hills, Deep Forest,
A decent soundtrack,
and my head on your knee.

Feeling the sun gently break through the trees
to shine upon the face that calms my Chaos.

Not needing to think talk or even look,
To Know Your Soul by feel,
to hear your thoughts without an utterance from
your lips.

Lazy Sunday,
Coffee,
Toast,
Robes,
Books,
Summer Rain,
Knowing peace and contentment.

Random drive to Nowhere,
Loud music,
Passion overtaking,
Stars,
Sex,
and lying there free.

Doing dishes,
Hands upon my hips,
Kisses on my neck.

Adventure and Pause,
Pulse and Peace,
Enchanted and Free

These are all the things I wish for,
You see.

Heaven Sent

Enthrall me again my lover,
Take me to The Tempest Sea,
Allow me to drink of your spirit,
Set Me Free

Undress Me With Your Eyes,
speak only from these,
Do not taint love with words
or mere mortal understanding.

Remember me always from those lives now gone,
I know you know my spirit from Heavenly days
But for now let's be as we always were, afire,
aflame, the Spark immutable.

You are a force to be reckoned with,
I shudder in anticipation of your kiss,
I know you will growl, I know I will expire,
I don't know how long I can hold this longing at
bay.

I desire your touch in so many ways,
Just sit with me, my friend and I will be content,
to know you exist is enough.
So allow my delight and soul to cherish, even if
you will never know.

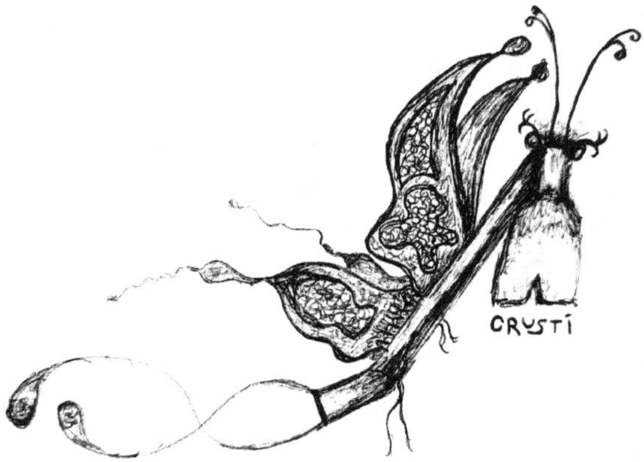
CRUSTI

When the scars Hum

I feel you all around as I stumble,
fall and cautiously walk,
love knocking on the door,
and fear once again looking at me,
"You can't let love in,
you know what happens, they will hurt you."

No one honours love,
they honour with their lips,
but not their hearts.

They take the gift of love for themselves,
hungry, devouring, sucking it dry.
Til I am left an empty husk trying to find my
feet again.

I don't know if I want to refill my cup,
they drink it dry.
Being unfulfilled makes others stay away,
there is nothing to take here.

It's safer this way no depth no her no desire.
But it's empty and so very lonely,
I want to shine as I used to,
but is it really worth the hurt?

Saving the Princess

Exhale love,
No one is coming to save you,
No one's going to give you a hug,
No one's going to wipe your tears,
You have to be your own superhero.

No one is ever going to truly hold you, Dear.
Everybody disappears - you'll never have a constant.
You're never going to fit and it doesn't matter.
No one is ever going to truly know you,
No one will rescue you,
You are alone.

And you know what, Princess,
it's going to be ok,
You can save yourself,
You know how to swim. xxx

You/Me

You or me used to be you and me.
The moment you know when it's changed,
the moment they ask for that last little piece of
yourself.

The quiet voice that calls you, "Don't you
remember how you feel when it was just you."
They ask for the compromise.

They dictate to you all you could be,
Just don't be too loud it hurts me.
Fit in this box and do not shake me.

But I was born to fly and dance,
If you want to belong and be a part of -
Please extinguish your sparkly self we have no
time for depth.

I'm sorry to inform you that I cannot stay,
I cannot fit and shine.
A star contained becomes a black hole,
so I choose me and leave you to you.

The arrogant and the Broken

If I could list the deception out loud,
The deception of my entire,
The deception of my truth,
There lies within me death howl,
An agonising scream,
To pierce the very fabric of existence,
You were the love so true,
That penetrated the depths of my soul,
Held me enthralled so much so,
I gladly gave you all,
Willingly,
But now I wonder why I cannot breathe.
To Exhale is to see,
I'll never show it but fuck man,
You broke me.
But that's OK sunshine,
I've been broken before,
I'm showing all your scars The Door.

Refinement Through Fire

What do you know of sacrifice?
What understanding true commitment,
What do you know of my true journey,
Of being broken to be refined.

Thinking it's done to be thrown into the fire,
Finding your feet to have them taken away
again.

So I will fight,

I will strive,

I know how precarious this life is.

So I will soak in every moment that I am in it.
I don't know how long until
I'm thrown down again,
But I will have made the best memories.

Velvet Lips

She has eyes that speak of mischief,
The night sky, and Destiny.
Lips that speak unbidden lust,
Hidden just for you to taste,
Lustrous sheen on auburn hair,
Skin of alabaster.

She is the Embodiment of Feminine,
Wrapped up in enough sass to stroke your soul,
and make you want nothing else but her time.
When you are with her no other exists,
when her hand strokes your face she has you encapsulated,
You willingly offer your soul
And anything else she desires.

She is Lilith and Eve,
The Fire and the Love.
But be wary, boys
Because she'll never be yours alone,
You can taste the pie
But never have the cake.

Traverse

I saw him,
The man who inspires and lightens my soul,
The unattainable, the rich and the vibrant,
Yet again, I am fruitless against my heart,
Beauty that cannot be captured and held,
He traverses past my soul again and again.

I am the holder of all the secrets,
But not the woman you want to grow old with,
Cannot allow yourself to collapse into the arms
of the voluptuous mind.

She won't buckle under your spell,
She holds her own and knows herself,
Darling boy, a lexicon of verbal magnitude does
not render me still,
The overdeveloped soul does not sink into
intelligence,
Too bad your fear stopped you from touching the
sun,
Unlearn your lies and accept your soul,
Come see me when you're complete and no
longer fear,
Waiting for you, would be the slow death of my
joy.

Goddess

Saying all I have to say,
Getting it off my chest,
How to breathe whilst suffocating,
To plead for your own stand,
While not losing your mind,
To be all that you want to be,
And not leave anyone behind.

I am unbelted and strong but vulnerable too.
I don't know how to find the words,
To truly put it out in the ether,
My emotions feel like napalm on the water,
Swirly, pretty to look at, with all its
resplendent iridescence.

But one little spark,
just one little flame,
This whole bitch will blow,
I might even enjoy watching it burn.
I was always a pagan deep inside,
I like fire even if it's me burning.

Quiet Hope

There's always a quiet hope in the morning after
I have dreams of you once again,
you live inside my heart and my mind.
I cannot find the words to express this to you
there's always this moment when you smile at
me as our eyes lock for a moment and I'm
absolutely devastated inside, that for you, I shall
never be the woman you desire.

Your love for me is pure, your eyes dance with a
mischief inside,
I'm lost and found all at once.
Your hand in mine is a place of safety,
Your arms contain the warmest embrace I have
ever felt,
You do not require me to be anything other than
me,
and I appreciate you more than you'll ever know.

But now for the silence, the moment ends.
For you shall never know for I would never do
anything to lose the love of my life.

Writing on the Wall

There it is again,
That moment when they looked at me,
Maybe I laughed too loud,
Maybe I love too hard but here it is again,
The Familiar withdraw,
suddenly busyness abounds and no time is found.
Clearly I see the perpetual fade,
The writing on the wall is so enamoured to me.
I've seen it so often that rejection has become my friend.

It never leaves, never fades but I refuse to change,
I could stop it in an instant but I will not succumb to dimming my light,
stifling my passion, so I'll look to the writing on the wall,
see that while they are rejecting,
I have kept me.

The Insatiable Need

I feel it again the tearing of my flesh,
wanting,
needing,
an embrace unfelt,
I search for you while lying to myself,
Make eye contact with strangers,
hoping something is awakened,
Where are you, my love?
Are you searching for me?

Are you wishing to find me,
to tear at my flesh,
To feed this insatiable need,
The one in the covers we no one can see,
The moulding of bodies, of steam and fire,
The resolute moment when all is expired,
and no more can be felt,
Till then I'll sit and dream of you to satisfy my
Insatiable Need.

Music Box

It's late, love.
The door is closed.
The music is all done,
Don't come around here, no more.
There isn't anything for you,
Just a Silent Night with no sleep,
I need to close the chapter and empty the barrel of tears.
I cannot heal thee,
I can't save me.
All I can do is listen till the song of solitude is my only friend,
All I can do is listen to the music,
I'm hoping for some words, some beat that will bring me back to me.
Cast adrift on the ocean of emotion,
Waiting to see,
Will it drown me or will my utterments fall to the ocean floor,
Making friends with the Titanic.
My Heart shall become the Heart of the Ocean.
Lost Forever and Never Found but you'll never know because glass reflects just as well as diamond.

Stardust

Love is a word that is thrown so carelessly,
So many people never know
what it truly means to me.
I tell many people that I love them
and it pauses on them,
I watch it.
They decide where in them it belongs,
In what context that it makes them feel safe,
Friend, Family, Lover, Stranger,
Weird woman expressing inappropriately,
You want to know a secret?
A little truth that no one knows,
Come closer lean in and truly feel these words,
I'm not talking to you here,
I'm talking to the stardust this
whole universe is made of,
Because if I love the Stardust inside me,
How could I not love the Stardust inside you?
So decide if you must where that love lies here,
But when we turn to the dust,
I'll love you there.

The Final Dance

A tattered Crown and a broken shoe, this world
was never meant for you.
You are the angel incarnate,
one of beauty and vibrant song.
Nevermind how they treat you,
it's not here you belong.
You are Stardust my dear you always ring true.
So dance freely my love the universe will hold
you.

I know there are days you are tired and I know
that there are times where you have tried.
But do not fear and do not worry it will all come
to be as it was meant to be this whole time,
all of this pain is refinement for you
to finally see the beautiful soul that is
encapsulated within, you cannot misstep,
Your God is near.

When you look back when you're 80 years old,
do you think you will worry about the day they
didn't call, the night that you spent wondering if
you will ever be enough?
Do you think that you will really be stuck on
how you didn't do that thing you were meant to

do that perfect way or do you think that you will
look at all of your days and smile with great
gladness for you have felt, lived, dreamed,
wandered, found, traversed, experienced and
loved,

So I know for all the days are just too much and
you just need a moment to sit,
Sit with me my dear and I will tell you these
dreams.
The one's of you dancing freely, loving holding,
traversing, stomping and gloriously flying
through this life and you do not need to worry
my love, it will all come true,
I promise you and the only way that you'll ever
see it, is if you go through it first.

So my parting wishes as this little book of
poems comes to an end is that hopefully I have
made you feel something and hopefully you'll
see the hope in the end.
That life will always give you ups and downs,
that it wouldn't be life without a roller-coaster
and occasional screaming sound.
So take my love and all my best wishes and
everything inside me.
I hope to see you as we trudge.

And Don't Forget to fall in love.

With Her, Him, They, Life, Art,
or the
scariest one of All,
Yourself. xxx

www.ingramcontent.com/pod-product-compliance
Lightning Source LLC
Chambersburg PA
CBHW051745130826
49812CB00033B/1010
* 9 7 8 9 3 5 7 2 1 2 9 1 5 *